Friends

making them & keeping them

by Patti Kelley Criswell
illustrated by Stacy Peterson

★ American Girl®

Editorial Development: Darcie Johnston, Michelle Watkins, Erin Falligant
Art Direction & Design: Jessica Meihack
Production: Jeannette Bailey, Judith Lary, Kristi Lively, Paula Moon
Illustrations: Stacy Peterson

Dear Reader,

At American Girl we understand how important
it is to have friends you can count on.

Inside we've given you everything you need to know
about making new friends and making the most of the
friendships you already have. You'll find tips,
quizzes, and even advice and stories from girls just like you.

Having friends who are really right for you is what it's
all about. That means finding friends who understand
and appreciate you for who you are. We hope
this book helps you do just that.

Your friends at American Girl

Contents

Making Friendships Last 36

Celebrating Friendship 64

Making Friends

Making a new friend takes time and even a little courage,
but it's worth it because good friends are like . . .

★ **a sunny day.** (Friends make life happier.)

★ **an umbrella in the rain.** (Friends make gloomy days more comfy.)

★ **a pile of autumn leaves.** (Friends make everything more fun.)

Friend Finders ✵

Sometimes it just takes being in the right place at the right time to find a friend. Get involved in activities you enjoy, and you'll improve your chances of meeting someone to enjoy them with.

✵ Play a sport

Join the team! Regular practices and exciting games and events can lead to close friendships. If competitive team sports aren't your thing, consider ice skating, tae kwon do, or even fencing.

✵ Take a class

What have you always wanted to try? Swimming? Cooking? Drawing or yoga or horseback riding? You'll be surrounded by people to meet, and you'll learn something new!

✵ Start something

What are you into? If it's reading, start a book club. If it's chess, start a chess club. If it's dance, start a dance club. Try to get girls together who like the same thing, and it's almost sure to pay off. Ask your teacher, librarian, or coach to help you get something going.

✵ Join a club

In after-school groups such as service clubs, scouts, or student council, you'll work on projects together and, chances are, find friends, too.

✵ Just get out of the house!

Watch for opportunities to get together with girls in your community, neighborhood, church, or school. Sign up for a 5K fun run or bake-sale booth to benefit a good cause. Participate in a park cleanup or school fund-raiser. Put yourself in situations where you can meet people, and hey, you just might!

Conversation Starters

When it comes to making new friends, someone has to start the conversation. Here are some good ways to get talking:

Find something in common
I saw you at the concert. Do you like jazz, too?

Offer to help
I can show you where that classroom is.

Just introduce yourself!
Hi! I'm Alisha. I think we're in the same class.

Show an interest
I've been wanting to read that book. Do you like it?
Give a compliment
I like your haircut. It looks great!
Share a little
I moved once, too, so I know it's really hard at first.
Ask an opinion
What do you think of the new soccer uniforms?
Offer an invitation
Want to sit together at lunch?

Keep the conversation going!

Once you've had a conversation, don't let it stop there. Look for chances to talk again. The more you talk, the more you'll get to know if this girl might be a good friend for you.

Could someone be trying to talk to you?

You might be thinking so much about starting a conversation with one girl that you don't notice another girl trying to start a conversation with *you*. Chances are, someone out there wants to get to know you better, too!

When You Feel Shy

Sometimes walking up to someone you don't know feels like a big deal. It can be really hard. And to make it even harder, shyness can sometimes be confusing for other girls who want to get to know you.

She's not talking to me. Is she just feeling shy? Or does that mean she doesn't want to be friends with me?

Meeting new friends when you feel shy can be a challenge. It's kind of like climbing up a big mountain. But taking it step by step really helps. Just remember that with every step you take and every effort you make, no matter how small, you're getting closer to meeting some great girls and enjoying fun friendships.

Saying Hello

Here are a few tips to help make saying hi easier.

Let your body help you do the talking.

It's hard to have a conversation with a girl whose head is down or whose arms are crossed tightly across her chest. But looking someone in the eye, and keeping your head up and your arms relaxed, tells other kids you'd like to talk to them. Taking a deep breath and smiling helps, too.

Approach one person instead of a whole group.

Act as natural as you can. You might also try bringing extra pens, paper, or gum along with you. Offering to share is a great way to start talking to someone.

Get those first words out.

Don't wait until you feel totally comfortable to approach someone. Just say something simple like, "Hi. How are you?" It may be easier than you think to go from there. Remember, most people are happy when someone shows an interest in them and what they have to say.

Practice at home in front of a mirror.

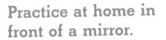

Act like you're talking to someone you've never met. It might sound silly, but it works! Once you've said the words out loud over and over, saying them to someone else won't be as difficult.

Ask your mom or dad to help you practice, practice, practice.

The more you practice starting conversations, the more natural it will feel. Try out conversation starters at the dinner table with your family. Ordering at restaurants and asking questions of salespeople can help, too. After a while, it won't seem so hard.

Advice from Girls

Here's what real girls had to say about making new friends:

"Walk up to someone who is alone, not with a group of friends. She will be glad someone is talking to her!"

SARAH, AGE 10

"Making friends is a lot like doing a jigsaw puzzle. Some people fit in a certain place and others don't. Just don't try to force it."

RYAN, AGE 14

"I try my best to be kind, honest, and loyal. Then I just trust that friendships will happen, and so far they have."

ELIZABETH, AGE 11

"I sit back and watch people for a while. If they seem nice from a distance, then I start talking to them."

NATALIE, AGE 9

"I love to laugh. I try to meet people who have a good sense of humor."

COURTNEY, AGE 13

"Don't judge people by what other people say about them. Get to know them, and then decide for yourself!"

SAM, AGE 13

"The number one thing about making friends is to be yourself. Don't try to be someone you're not. People won't respect you if they think you're a faker."

AMANDA, AGE 13

19

Trying Too Hard

When it comes to making and keeping friends, one thing that doesn't work is *clinging*. Friendships can end *fast* when one girl feels overwhelmed by the other. In other words, don't try too hard!

What rates high on the cling-o-meter?

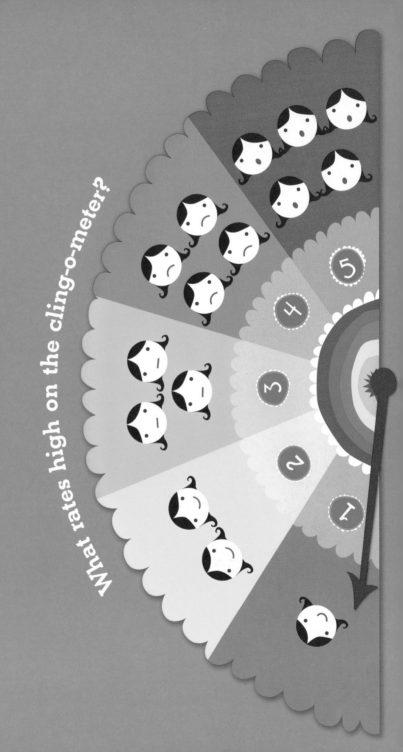

cling-o-meter rating:

You meet your new friend on Monday. On Wednesday, you ask her to be your best friend.

When friendships are new, it's important to let them grow naturally. Don't rush into making the friendship more than it is. For now, just focus on getting to know your friend better.

cling-o-meter rating:

You've been friends for a few months. For four weeks in a row, you've spent your allowance on presents for your new friend.

Careful. Your presents may make your friend feel too much pressure, and that could change an otherwise good friendship. Also, you won't know whether your friend likes you for *you* or for all the gifts you give her. So cool it on the spending, and think of other ways to let your friend know you care about her.

cling-o-meter rating:

Your friend has told you she can't come over, but you really, really want her to. You don't understand why she doesn't want to come over, so you call her—again and again.

Take a deep breath. Respect is a key part of friendship, and you're not respecting your friend's wishes. Give her some space, and invite another friend over instead.

cling-o-meter rating:

You see your friend out bike riding with another girl. You're so upset that you cry for an hour and refuse to talk to her the next morning on the bus.

Just because she has other friends doesn't mean she doesn't care for you, and refusing to talk to her is more likely to hurt your friendship than make it better. Instead, reassure yourself that your friend is still your friend, and remind yourself that you have other friends, too.

Circle of Friends

Rather than searching for that one perfect pal, surround yourself with many friends. You'll bring out the best in one another!

Do you dream of that one perfect best friend—the girl who will meet your every friendship need?

The truth is, no one person can meet all your needs. Besides, that's way too much pressure to put on one person.

Instead of waiting and hoping for the perfect friend to come along, how about trying to build a circle of friends? Don't limit yourself to people who seem just like you. Maybe there's an older or younger girl in your neighborhood you'd like to get to know better—or even a boy you've met.

Be open to all kinds of friendships. One friend might be great at listening but not like the same hobbies you like. And you might have another friend who's really fun but isn't so easy to be serious with.

How do you know if someone will be a good friend? At first, you don't. One girl may look or dress like you, but when you're with her, it just doesn't feel right. Another girl may seem totally different from you, but you feel like you can really be yourself with her.

Just remember, each of your friends is a unique person with a unique place in your life. What's most important is that you—and all of your friends—really enjoy each other.

All Kinds of Friends

Try your best to build a good balance of buds.

True-blue friend

This friend has seen you at your best and your worst, and she loves you just the same. You can talk to her about anything at any time, or you can just sit silently with her and still feel comfortable.

True-blue friend qualities

- ★ Great for a pep talk
- ★ You feel 100 percent comfortable when you're with her
- ★ Picks you up when you're down
- ★ Won't judge you
- ★ Knows you inside and out

Giggling girl

This friend is just plain fun! When you're with her, the two of you laugh at the silliest things. And if you're feeling down, she'll have you cheered up in no time.

Giggling girl qualities

- ★ Helps you laugh (and laugh and laugh . . .)
- ★ Takes a bad situation and turns it around by making you smile
- ★ Turns the most boring activity into something fun

Go-to girl

Every girl needs someone she can turn to when she needs some advice. Maybe this special friend is your big sister, your neighbor, or a family friend. She tells you what she thinks is best for you, even if it's not what you want to hear. She always helps you feel that everything will be OK.

Go-to girl qualities

★ Honest and straightforward when giving you advice

★ 100 percent trustworthy

★ Has a good perspective on any problems you have

★ Cares about what's best for you

Casual pal

This friend shares an interest with you. Maybe you're on the same soccer team or take guitar lessons together. The two of you might hang out only at your shared activities, but when you're together, it's great. Just make sure you don't keep score on who's better at whatever you have in common. Be supportive, and keep it fun.

Casual pal qualities

★ Shares your interests

★ Gets you outside of your normal group of friends

★ Motivates you to practice or work on your activity

Delightfully different friend

There's never a dull moment with this friend because she isn't just like you. Maybe she's from a different culture, or maybe this friend is a boy. This friend challenges you to be creative and try new things.

Delightfully different friend qualities

- ★ Has interests that are not the same as yours
- ★ Encourages you to try new ways of doing things
- ★ Makes you think, "Oh, I never thought of it that way!"

Faraway friend

You and this girl have stayed close, even though she's far away. You don't have to talk every day to stay friends, but hearing from her makes you smile. You always pick up right where you left off, and if you get to visit each other, it's nothing but fun!

Faraway friend qualities

- ★ Helps you learn about life in a different place
- ★ Brightens your day with an e-mail or a postcard
- ★ Brings a fresh and fair perspective to your problems since she isn't involved and doesn't know all your friends

Close-to-home friend

This friend might be a sibling, a cousin, a parent, or a grandparent. Because she's part of your family, you might not even think of her as a friend. Our family members are our *forever* friends.

Close-to-home friend qualities

- ★ Is always there
- ★ Knows you inside and out
- ★ Has known you longer than your other friends
- ★ Loves you no matter what!

Furry friend

This friend might be your pet dog, your neighbor's cat, or even your favorite stuffed animal. No matter what this friend is, it's the one who listens to you and never judges you. Your "FF" might not give you any advice, but one look at that fuzzy face makes you smile.

Furry friend qualities

- ★ Never tells your secrets
- ★ Comes when you call
- ★ Stays by your side

Getting to Know Her

Learning more about each other can help you decide whether your friendship will flourish or fizzle. But sometimes when you're getting to know a person, it's hard to find things to talk about. Avoid awkward moments by playing the getting-to-know-you games on the next few pages.

BIG IMPORTANT POINT

When you first meet someone, try hard NOT to rely on gossip to fill up the conversation. It might be tempting, but it almost always backfires and sends a message to your new friend that you're not very trustworthy.

Things About Me

Instructions:

★ Find a deck of playing cards. Remove all the 6s through the 10s, and keep the aces through 5s, the face cards, and the jokers.

★ Take turns picking a card from the deck. The number on the card tells you how many interesting facts about yourself to share. If you pick a 3, you might say:

"I once rode an elephant."

"I love to swim."

"I have a rock collection."

★ If you pick the joker, ask your friend a question of your choice.

★ If you pick a face card, answer a question from your friend or from the next page.

BIG IMPORTANT POINT

Nobody should have to answer a question she finds too embarrassing. You always have the option to say "pass."

Twenty Questions

Instructions:

★ Make a copy of these two pages, or write the questions on a sheet of paper.

★ Cut the paper so that each question is on its own little slip.

★ Put the slips in a bowl—or any fun container.

★ Take turns pulling out a slip, reading the question out loud, and answering it. You can both answer the same question, or each of you can pull a new slip when it's your turn.

1. What is something you are scared of?

2. What's your favorite thing to do on the weekend?

3. Tell about your earliest memory.

4. What is your favorite part of the school day?

5. What's your favorite place to visit?

6. If you were given a million dollars, what would you do with it?

7. Describe a family tradition that you really enjoy.

8. Name one great thing about your family.

9. If you could go anywhere in the world you've never been, where would it be?

10. Tell about your greatest adventure ever.

11. What's your favorite kind of music?

12. What book character is most like you? Why?

13. What is your favorite food?

14. If you could be any animal, what would you be?

15. If you could change your name, what would it be?

16. What is your dream job?

17. Name something you've always wanted to do but haven't had the chance to do yet.

18. What is your all-time favorite movie?

19. Who is the most inspiring person you know? Why?

20. What three, four, or five words best describe you?

This or That?

Instructions:

★ Make two copies of this game or write the pairs of words on a sheet of paper—one for you and one for your new friend.

★ For each pair, circle the thing you like better, while she does the same on her copy.

★ Read your answers to each other, circling the other's favorites in a different pen color.

★ Have fun talking about how you're the same—and how you're different!

winter
or
summer

ice cream
or
french fries

shopping
or
slumber parties

swimming
or
running

dogs
or
cats

print book
or
e-book

art class
or
gym class

hotels
or
camping

sports events
or
plays

in-line skating
or
biking

on the stage
or
in the audience

pants
or
skirts

board games
or
card games

talking it out
or
writing it down

the movie
or
the book

sneakers
or
flip-flops

True Friendship Story

"A real friend is one who walks in
when the rest of the world walks out."
—WALTER WINCHELL

I hadn't been in class with Emma for very long because she moved up to our grade and joined our class late. She seemed nice, but we never got to know each other. To be honest, I was a little scared by how smart she was. I mean, she skipped a whole grade!

Anyway, we were in class, and I was reading aloud in our small group. I accidentally missed a word. It had a weird ending, and I didn't read it the right way.

That's when Maggie, another girl in my group, embarrassed me by saying loudly, "The word is *buffet*. Duh! You didn't know *buffet?*"

I felt so bad, I just wanted to run away.

Just then, out of nowhere, Emma piped up and said, "Maggie, that's mean. Everybody

misses words. *Buffet* is hard." I was stunned. The whole group was stunned. And Maggie, who is used to getting away with rude comments, was stunned, too.

Just then, our teacher had everyone in the class go back to their seats. I mouthed "thank you" to Emma.

After that, I couldn't wait until lunch to really thank her. I let her know how much I respected her for what she had done. We played all recess and most recesses after that. She's still one of the best friends I have ever had.

—AN AMERICAN GIRL

P.S. Maggie was a lot less rude from then on, too.

Making Friendships Last

Being friends is like riding a bicycle. Sometimes the ride feels smooth and easy. Other times you have to climb uphill or you hit a bump in the road. That's OK. Every road has a few hills and bumps. You can't avoid them completely, but if you know how to handle them—when to pedal harder, how to steer—you can usually stay on the right path. And in the end, a great friendship is worth the ride.

Top Ten Trouble Starters

You won't be able to avoid every fight with your friends. You'll have fewer fights, though, if you steer clear of these trouble starters.

 Talking about someone behind her back

 Asking a friend to take sides and choose between you and another friend

 Breaking a promise or telling a secret

4 Being bossy

5 Bragging or showing off

6 Leaving someone out—and letting her know it in a mean way

 7 Being jealous of or competing with your friend

 8 Saying something unkind about your friend or her loved ones

 9 Embarrassing your friend in front of others

 10 Being too busy to listen

What Listening Looks Like

It's easy to do the talking when your friend is a good listener, but being a good listener takes practice. Think of a conversation as being like a ride on a teeter-totter. Have you ever been on a teeter-totter that doesn't seem to go up and down? That's how it feels when one person does a lot more of the talking. It's out of balance—and not that much fun.

A good conversation goes something like this:

First your friend shares . . .

. . . and then you comment on what she shared so that she knows you were listening . . .

Listening Tips

Keep these helpful hints in mind the next time you talk with a friend.

★ **Listen to your friend.** When she is talking, make sure your eyes are on her and your brain is paying attention to her words. It's so easy to focus on what you want to say next, but instead, keep your focus on her.

★ **Try not to interrupt.** It can be tempting to jump in, but no one likes feeling cut off. If you don't understand something, wait for her to finish, and then ask a question.

★ **Consider her point of view.**
Try not to judge your friend, even if you don't agree with how she's handling a problem.

★ **Offer support** with comments such as, "Wow, that must have made you really mad" or "You must have been so happy!"

Sometimes, when a friend has a serious problem, you might need to do lots of listening and less sharing. This is OK as long as it doesn't happen all the time. When your friend does need you, listen to her. It's comforting to know that she'll do the same for you, too, when you need her.

Building Trust

Promise you won't tell anyone?

When someone tells you something private, it's as if they're giving you a compliment. They are telling you that they trust you and value your opinion.

If someone trusts you with confidential information, keep it private. If you don't, you risk losing one of the most important parts of a friendship—trust.

When two people trust each other, they have opened the doors for their friendship to grow stronger. If you break your friend's trust, it's like slamming that door shut.

Think about it: Do you really want to trade the respect of your friend for a moment of attention? People may like to hear gossip, but the truth is, they don't trust—or respect—the person spreading it. So if someone trusts you enough to share something personal with you, keep it just to yourself.

BIG
IMPORTANT POINT

There is only one exception to this rule: If your friend is in danger, you need to tell someone—an adult, not your other friends. It's always the right decision to keep a friend safe. Even if she's upset at first, in the end she'll know that you were looking out for her and that you cared.

Being There

A big part of friendship is being in your friend's corner when she needs you. Here are two ways to stick up for a friend when other kids are giving her trouble.

I can't believe you just said that!

1. Let the others know with words that it's not OK to pick on your friend. This works especially well if you have the support of your other friends, too. And while it may seem daring and even scary to stand up to a rude classmate, it shows that you're a strong person and a loyal friend.

2. **Let a grown-up know** that your friend is being picked on, if standing up to a classmate doesn't feel comfortable. Tell the grown-up that you're concerned for your friend, and give examples of what you have seen happening.

If talking to a grown-up seems too big a step, you could write an anonymous note or even ask your parents to talk to someone for you. One way or another, let the people in charge know what's happening so that they can take care of it.

Ms. King, I'm worried about my friend. She has been getting bullied by . . .

Ms. Munoz, I think you should know about something . . .

Telling or Tattling?

It can be hard to know what to do when you see your friend being bullied. For each of these bully problems, should you tell? Or would you just be tattling? Write down or circle your choice.

Problem 1.

Jane keeps teasing your friend Kasia. She's been doing it all week. You want to say something to the playground supervisor.

TELLING
or
TATTLING

Problem 2.

You've tried to stand up for Penny when Jon makes fun of her in gym class, but it's not working, and now Penny is skipping gym. You want to report Jon to the gym teacher.

TELLING
or
TATTLING

Problem 3.

Ian has nice things—his shoes, his backpack, his jacket. A group of girls make rude comments every day, and he just takes it, but you can see it bothers him. You want to tell the school counselor.

TELLING

or

TATTLING

Problem 4.

Your friend Madison completely shuts down when Rachel says something mean to her. You wish Madison could stand up for herself, but she just can't—and you're afraid of Rachel, too. You want to talk to your teacher about it.

TELLING

or

TATTLING

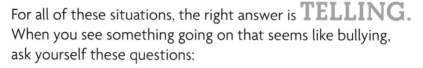

For all of these situations, the right answer is TELLING. When you see something going on that seems like bullying, ask yourself these questions:

★ Has the bullying happened more than once?

★ Do you feel like your friend can't stand up for herself?

★ Has anyone tried to stop the bully—but failed?

★ Is more than one person involved in the bullying?

If the answer to any of the questions is YES (as it is with each situation here), it's time to tell an adult.

BIG
IMPORTANT POINT

Tattling is done to make someone look bad. Telling is done to help someone. So ask yourself, does my friend need my help right now? If you don't know, ask her!

Remember:

If your friend is being bullied, this is a time she really needs you. Don't be afraid to let her know how much you disagree with the hurtful things that have been said.

Who cares if you're not like them? You're great the way you are! I'm really glad we're friends.

The way they act is their problem, not yours. Try not to let it get to you.

Don't listen to them. What they said was just mean.

Fighting Fair

Sometimes you can't avoid a fight. But do you know how to fight right?
Read each fighting strategy, and decide whether it's fair or unfair.
Write down or circle your choice.

1. If you talk really loudly and even cry, you'll get your point across better.

2. Talk about the problem to everyone except your friend. Get lots of people on your side so that your friend will give in faster.

3. Don't talk about why you're angry. You shouldn't have to tell your friend. She should already know.

4. When your friend is talking, don't focus on what she's saying. Instead, use the time to think about what you're going to say next.

5. Make sure you bring up everything your friend has ever done that bothers you— not just what you are unhappy about right now.

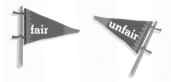

6. Try to forget it and stay out of her way. Even though what happened bothers you, the thought of talking about it with her is too upsetting.

7. The silent treatment is better than arguing. A cold shoulder will cause your friend to warm up fast!

Answers

How did you answer? If you said **UNFAIR** to all of the statements on the last page, you know that to untangle the knots and solve your friendship troubles you need a good attitude—and a few basic ground rules. Here they are:

1. Cool it. Shouting and tears will get a person's attention, but they also keep that person from understanding the real reason you're upset. Try to express yourself as calmly as you can. Remember: Words that are said in anger can really hurt, and hurtful words only make the problem bigger. Instead, cool down. Say what you mean and mean what you say, but don't say it mean.

2. Keep it private. Talking to others can help you sort out your feelings, but it's no substitute for talking directly to the person you're mad at. You don't want to put other friends in the middle of your argument with her, and she could feel betrayed if you tell other friends about it—making it even worse.

3. Say what's bothering you. Don't expect your friend to read your mind. She can't change or fix the problem if she doesn't know what it is. Ask a parent or another trusted adult (but not another friend—see #2!) to help you sort out your feelings if you need to. You'll be much better prepared when you do try to talk it out.

4. Pay attention. It's hard to listen when you're angry. But your friend may be trying to tell you something important that could change how you feel. If you hear it soon enough, you can often stop a fight before it gets worse.

BIG IMPORTANT POINT

Nobody's perfect. Everybody makes mistakes. If you expect your friends to be perfect, you'll always be disappointed. So if you're angry with a friend, ask yourself if she really meant to hurt you or if she just made a mistake. Ask yourself if you might have made one, too, by misunderstanding her or having unfair expectations.

5. **Stick to today.** Bringing up things from the past or starting up old arguments takes the attention away from what's happening now, and it only stirs up more bad feelings. Focus on solving just one problem at a time.

6. **Don't clam up.** Sometimes it's best to deal with what seems like small stuff and NOT just let it go. If you step back and take some time to think about the situation but it still bothers you the next day, then you need to take a deep breath and bring it up with your friend. In the end, it will be easier for you to truly put the problem behind you.

7. **Forget the freeze.** Ignoring someone as a way to get even or to get her to apologize is not just unfair, it's mean—and it can ruin a friendship. Instead of going silent, face your friend and tell her how you feel about what happened.

Talking It Out

Are you ready to hear each other out? If so, all you need is a quiet place and the willingness to work together. Remember these helpful hints:

1. Don't be afraid to make the first move. One of the hardest parts about fixing things after a fight is getting started. Taking the lead doesn't mean you're giving in or letting your friend "win." Nobody wins if you never speak again.

Here are some ways to get the conversation started:

I'm ready to talk if you want to.

I feel terrible about how we ended things.

I'm still angry, but I care about our friendship and want to work things out.

Notice that all the sentences start with "I." That's because you're sharing your feelings—not telling her what she should have done differently. Using "I" statements gets the conversation off to a good start.

2. **Take turns talking.** The more you listen to your friend, the more she'll want to listen to you. Agree to take turns so that you both get a chance to say what's on your mind.

3. **Name the problem.** Keep using "I" statements. These are *your* feelings you're talking about. And try to avoid saying the words "you always" or "you never." Chances are, those statements aren't true, and they will just make your friend angry.

4. **Put yourself in your friend's place.** You know how you feel, but try to understand why she acted the way she did.

5. **Make an agreement about how to handle things in the future.** Maybe you've learned something about each other. Try to figure out what that is so that you don't have the same fight again.

6. **You can agree to disagree.** You might both be sorry about what happened and still not agree on everything. It's OK to have different opinions.

BIG
IMPORTANT POINTS

1. It's almost always worth it to try to work things out. When friends stick together through bumpy times, they have the chance to become truly *great* friends.

2. Even if you decide that you and your friend aren't a great match after all, you can still remain friends—just maybe not as close as you once thought. Not every friend has to be a BFF.

Making Things Right

If a problem between friends is very small, a simple "Sorry about that!" might be enough to get things back to normal. But if the fight between you and your friend is a big one—and you're the one who needs to apologize—take a deep breath and do it with words that are clear and from the heart.

Follow these simple rules for saying you're sorry:

★ **Say the words:** "I'm sorry for . . ."

★ **Reassure your friend** that you won't repeat the mistake, and let her know what you wish you had done instead: "I won't do that again. Next time I'll . . ."

★ **Ask what you can do.** Let her know that the friendship means a lot to you and that you want to make things right: "Is there anything I can do to make you feel better?"

Never be too proud to ask for forgiveness—or too stubborn to give it. If someone asks you to forgive her, she's done what she can to make things right. If you need to apologize for your part in the argument, do it. Then put the fight behind you and start rebuilding your friendship.

True Friendship Story

"The only way to have a friend is to be one."
—RALPH WALDO EMERSON

Danielle and I were on the same gymnastics team. We spent long hours together at the gym and got along great. *Finally,* I thought, *the friendship I've always dreamed of.*

Then one day everything changed.

New levels for gymnastics teams came out, and Danielle moved up a level. I didn't. I was crushed and cried all afternoon. I felt sure the days of our perfect friendship were over. I blamed myself for not being a better gymnast.

I felt hurt and even angry at Danielle for being able to do more in the gym. To make matters worse, it was becoming clear that gymnastics just wasn't for me, and I ended up dropping from the team altogether.

Then one lonely afternoon, the phone rang. It was Danielle saying how much she missed our friendship. I was so happy because I had missed her, too. We got together that day and came up with a plan to build back our friendship. We even asked our moms for help. Now Danielle's mom drops her off at my house in the morning so that we can walk to school together.

We've worked hard to find time to be together, and as a result, our friendship has grown. In fact, it's stronger than it's ever been. For us, gymnastics brought us together, but true friendship—and determination— kept us that way.

—AN AMERICAN GIRL

Celebrating Friendship

Think of a friendship as being like a beaded necklace. Every experience you and your friend have together—every memory you make—is like a bead. Bead by bead, the two of you create something beautiful. And like a precious necklace, your friendship is something you'll cherish and want to take care of.

Showing You Care

Friendship is a two-way street—you care for her and she cares for you back. Here are some great ways to show your friend how much she matters.

Wish her good luck on a test.

Call her to keep in touch, especially through busy times.

Be nice to her brothers and sisters.

Help make her birthday special.

Return what you borrow from her.

Let her teach you something new.

Give her a pep talk if she needs it.

Teach her to do something you know how to do.

Help her clean her room.

Tell her why you admire her.

Notice if she gets her hair cut.

Save her a seat.

If you have something good in your lunch, share it!

Invite her over.

If you know she collects something—say, snow globes—and you see one, get it for her.

Be reliable and on time.

Listen without judging.

SEASON'S GREETINGS

Say thank you when she does something nice.

Stop her if she's putting herself down.

Remember her favorite things.

If she forgets her mittens, give her one of yours.

Share your umbrella if she doesn't have one.

Tell her a joke to make her laugh.

69

Friendship Ties

The more time you spend with a friend, the more opportunities you have to create lasting memories. Over time, you'll develop certain things you and your friend often do together. These traditions become an important part of your friendship, strengthening the bond between the two of you.

Want to start some traditions with a friend?

Here's how:

1 **Pick something you both love to do.** It could be something as simple as watching the same TV show and talking about it, or doing something special for each other's birthdays. Maybe it's going to the same place together once a year.

2 **Remember the tradition.** The activity you're sharing with your friend can become a tradition only if you repeat it over and over, and that takes some *effort*. But that's also what makes it so special!

"Inside jokes" happen when friends who shared a funny moment are reminded of it later. These jokes are a fun way to bring back memories and enjoy a good laugh, but inside jokes can also make others feel left out. Unless you plan to let others in on the joke, avoid mentioning it when they're around.

Real Girls' Traditions

Here are some ideas from real girls.

"I have a friend who moved across town, but we still get to see each other because every spring we pick blueberries and every fall we pick apples. We always spend our birthdays together, too." GRACE, AGE 8

"Our tradition is called 'Sister Day.' My friend and I dress alike and pretend that we are sisters for the day." MORGAN, AGE 9

"My friend Annie and I always have tea parties in the spring, and we give each other little gifts and take pictures. In all the pictures, we are laughing and having fun!" KATIE, AGE 10

"When we were little, my friend and I had our picture taken together with our favorite tree every spring. Now that we are older, we still do that every year. It's fun to look back at the pictures and see how much we (and the tree!) have changed." NAN, AGE 9

"We met at summer camp and became postcard pals. Every time one of us sends a card, the other returns one right away." KATY, AGE 9, AND KELSEY, AGE 9

"Every summer, I go camping with my friend Isabel's family. We always go to the same campsite, and we each bring a new ghost story for the campfire the first night." LEAH, AGE 9

Friendship Fun

Try these ideas for keeping the fun in your friendship!

✳ Make a **time capsule** to open together a few years from now—three, five, or even ten years! Write down your dreams and predictions. Include a description of life as you know it. Put in letters from parents or friends, ticket stubs, and anything else that's important to you today. Seal it up and store it in a safe place!

✳ Write and publish a **blog or newsletter** for your friends and families. You can include stories, photos, artwork, poetry, jokes, and anything else that you and your friend—and your readers—find interesting!

✳ Write, direct, and produce **your own show**. Invite people you know to attend. Try to make a video of your production!

✴ Sign up to take part in a **charity race or walk.** Train for it together, and collect donations. Whether you're helping to find a cure for a disease or raising awareness of a problem in your area, you'll be making a difference!

✴ Start a **business** together. It could be weeding gardens or walking dogs. Create fun flyers, and ask your neighbors or others you know to be customers. Do something special with the money you earn!

✴ Make a **scrapbook.** Fill it with photos, drawings, and other mementos of your friendship.

✴ Invent your own **board game.** Have your friends and families try it out.

✴ Help each other **clean and organize your rooms.** You might even be able to rearrange the furniture—with a parent's permission, of course. With a friend's help, a big job is somehow easier and much more fun. Be sure to take "before" and "after" pictures!

Friendship Crafts

Get creative! Try these crafts with friends, or surprise them with a gift that celebrates your friendship.

Perfect Picture of Friendship

You'll need:

★ Pencil

★ Large piece of foam-core board

★ Patterned paper or ribbon

★ Glue

★ Pictures, quotes, and mementos

★ Sparkly stickers or plastic gemstones

★ Cord or yarn

★ Stapler or tape

1. Draw a faint line 1 to 3 inches in from each edge of the foam-core board. This marks your "frame." Glue ribbon or strips of brightly colored or patterned paper onto the frame.

2. In the middle of the frame, make a collage with pictures, quotes, and mementos of your friendship, such as movie tickets or school programs. Fill the gaps with stickers, gemstones, or other decorative items.

3. Tie a knot at each end of the cord or yarn. Turn the foam-core over, and center the cord at the top. Staple or tape both ends of the cord, just above the knots. Now hang up your masterpiece!

MARIAH   JORDAN   TAYLO

Sleepover Memory Pillow

You'll need:

★ Plain pillowcase

★ Cardboard

★ Fabric markers

★ Friendship quotes

★ Sparkly stickers

1. Place a piece of cardboard inside the pillowcase so that the marker will not bleed through to the other side.

2. Pull the pillowcase tightly across the cardboard. Use fabric markers to decorate the edges of the pillowcase with fun designs, such as stars, hearts, or flowers. Add quotes about friendship, if you like.

3. Leave room so that when friends sleep over, they can sign their names or write something about your friendship.

Note:

When you wash the pillowcase, follow the manufacturer's instructions on your fabric markers.

79

True Friendship Story

"Friendship is a sheltering tree."
—SAMUEL TAYLOR COLERIDGE

It was like any other day—I was at home, just hanging out, and I went to the garage to get something. When I opened the door, all I could see were flames! I was frantic! I ran to the neighbors. We called the fire department, but then all we could do was wait. I watched everything my family owned burn to the ground.

I was devastated. The sadness I felt is hard to describe. I was sad about so many things, but my mom says one of the first things I said was, "My doll. I lost my doll."

The next few days were kind of a blur, but one thing I remember is my friends. They just kept on coming, bringing us food and clothes.

But one friend really surprised me. It was two days after the fire, and my mom and I were rummaging through the remains of our house.

My friend Wendy walked up. She had moved a few months before and now lived two hours away. When our eyes met, I was overjoyed. I couldn't believe she had come all that way.

Wendy handed me a long box. When I opened it, my heart skipped a beat. It was Wendy's doll like mine and a whole bunch of clothes for her. "I want you to have her" was all she said. Then we hugged each other for a long time.

I was so touched, I didn't know what to say.

I will never forget the feeling I had that day or what Wendy did for me. The doll and my friend will always have a place in my heart.

—AN AMERICAN GIRL

Growing Friends

By now, you know how important friendship is. Next to our families, our friends know us best.

If you already have a circle of friends who make you happy, you are truly lucky. Cherish your friends and try to be the kind of friend you would want to have.

If you haven't found that great circle of friends yet, keep looking. Work to be the best friend you can be, and use what you've learned in this book to choose wisely and be patient while your friendships grow.

Remember: Some friendships will last a long time and others will fade away, but every friendship will teach you a little bit more about life and about the very best friend you have . . . you.

Good-Friend Checklist

Now that you've read this book, you know what it takes to make friends and to be a good friend. Are you being the best friend you can be? Write down or put a check next to every statement that sounds like you.

- [ ] I am reliable. When I say I'm going to do something, I do it.

- [ ] I try hard to be a good listener.

- [ ] I stick up for my friends when others say bad things about them.

- [ ] I let my friends get to know the real me.

- [ ] I refuse to say bad things about my friends, even when they make mistakes.

- [ ] If I am angry with a friend, I tell her and we work it out.

☐ When my friends put themselves down, I disagree with them.

☐ I ask for support when I need it.

☐ I am honest with my friends and say things in a kind way.

☐ If I hurt someone's feelings, I apologize.

☐ I keep my friends' personal information private.

How did you do?

Which areas of friendship are hardest for you? What do you need to do differently? Finish this sentence: "Starting today, I will be a better friend by . . ."

Do you have any tips for making friendships last?

How did you meet your best friends?

Do you have any ideas for making friendships last?

What special traditions do you share?

How do you handle it when you disagree?

WRITE TO US!
Send your true friendship stories to:

Friends **Editor**
American Girl
8400 Fairway Place
Middleton, WI 53562

Has your best friend ever moved away?

Here are some other American Girl books you might like:

Each sold separately. Find more books online at americangirl.com.

Parents, request a FREE catalog at **americangirl.com/catalog**.
Sign up at **americangirl.com/email** to receive the latest news and exclusive offers.

Discover online games, quizzes, activities,
and more at **americangirl.com/play**